is for blob.

Slimy, sticky, hungry – the blob eats everything in its path.
Plus, it's really hard to brush blob off your shoes.

C is for Cyclops.

This Ancient Greek monster has one enormous eye, instead of two. Cyclopes are giants. To them, people are tiny, tasty snacks.

4

D is for dark.

Many, many monsters disappear in the dark. Your wardrobe is pretty dark. But, hey, I'm sure there's nothing in there.

E is for eerie.

Have you ever seen something so strange that it made you shiver a little with fear? Maybe even in this book? That's so eerie.

F is for Frankenstein's monster.

In a famous story, mad scientist Victor Frankenstein creates a monster from several people's body parts. Remember, Frankenstein was the scientist, NOT the monster.

G is for gremlin.

Gremlins are like goblins or imps with a special mission to mess with machines. Is your computer crashing? Is your blender going berserk? It might be a gremlin.

H is for **headless horseman**.

A cannonball made this horseman headless during the American Revolutionary War. Now his ghost leaves his grave each night, galloping around looking for his lost head.

I is for imp.

Imps are small and rather ugly, but they usually won't hurt you. They make mischief and play pranks. These magical creatures are related to fairies, goblins and gremlins.

J is for jitters.

We're close to the middle of the book. Are you shaky and nervous about what's to come? You, my friend, may have the jitters.

K is for Kraken.

In old stories, the Kraken was a huge sea monster that looked like a giant squid. Sailors feared the Kraken. It could swallow ships!

L is for Loch Ness Monster.

The Loch Ness Monster is said to live in a deep, cold lake in Scotland called Loch Ness. Most people say Nessie looks like a plesiosaur, which died out millions of years ago. Or did it?

Human

Plesiosaur

 **is for mutant.**

There's more to mutants than meets the eye. Something about a mutant is not normal. Imagine a cockroach the size of a man. Or a pony with fangs and bat wings!

14

 **is for NOOOOOOO!!!**

Are you screaming, "Nooo! Stop! This is too scary!" dear reader? I'm sorry, but we're not done with the alphabet yet.

is for Ogre.

Ogres are oversized, ugly brutes. They have big appetites and odd tastes. One of their favourite snacks is children.

is for poltergeist.

Poltergeists are ghosts that can move things and mess with your TV! They've even been known to bite or pinch. Watch out!

17

is for quiet.

Quite a lot of monsters stomp, hiss or scream.
They're scary, but you can hear them coming.
Quiet monsters make no sound at all.

18

R is for roar.

Monsters that roar are usually beasts with big sharp teeth. When they roar, you get a close-up view of those chompers!

 **is for snake.**

Snakes can send shivers slithering right up your spine!
In Greek mythology, the monster Medusa had hair of hissing
snakes. One look at her could turn you to stone.

20

T is for troll.

Trolls are smaller than ogres, but just as ugly. They live underground or under bridges. You must be good at solving riddles if you want to cross a troll bridge.

U is for undead.

"Undead" means brought back to life from the dead. Ancient Egyptians turned people into mummies after they died. According to stories, mummies come back to life as undead monsters.

V is for vampire.

Speaking of undead ... vampires get to live forever. But they must drink blood to survive! They also must avoid sharp sticks in their hearts.

is for **werewolf.**

Werewolves are people who are cursed. They turn into wolves during the full moon. Is that a wolf howling at the moon? Or a WEREwolf?

X is for eXtraterrestrial.

"Extraterrestrial" is a big word for alien. It means "not of Earth". Aliens might look like little green men or giant creepy bugs. They usually want one thing – to take over the world!

Y is for Yeti.

Yetis are also known as Abominable Snowmen. They might be related to Bigfoots. They are big, hairy and white. Yetis blend in with the snowy mountains where they live.

Z is for zombie.

Zombies are the most famous undead monsters of all. Zombies are people who died and came back to life. The problem? Now they want to eat your brains! They are known to move slowly, so now's your chance. Run, dear reader, run!

INDEX

Raintree is an imprint of Capstone Global Library Limited, a company incorporated
in England and Wales having its registered office at 264 Banbury Road, Oxford, OX2 7DY –
Registered company number: 6695582

www.raintree.co.uk
myorders@raintree.co.uk

Text © Capstone Global Library Limited 2017
The moral rights of the proprietor have been asserted.

Designer: Ashlee Suker
Art Director: Nathan Gassman
Production Specialist: Katy LaVigne
The illustrations in this book were created digitally.

ISBN 978 1 4747 2445 6 (hardcover)
20 19 18 17 16
10 9 8 7 6 5 4 3 2 1

ISBN 978 1 4747 2449 4 (paperback)
21 20 19 18 17
10 9 8 7 6 5 4 3 2 1

British Library Cataloguing in Publication Data
A full catalogue record for this book is available from the British Library.

Every effort has been made to contact copyright holders of material reproduced in this book.
Any omissions will be rectified in subsequent printings if notice is given to the publisher.

All the Internet addresses (URLs) given in this book were valid at the time of going to press.
However, due to the dynamic nature of the Internet, some addresses may have changed, or sites may have
changed or ceased to exist since publication. While the author and publisher regret any inconvenience this
may cause readers, no responsibility for any such changes can be accepted
by either the author or the publisher.

Printed and Bound in China.

Other Titles in This Series

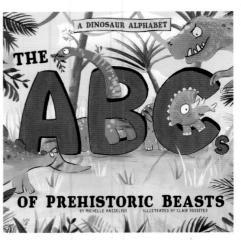

A DINOSAUR ALPHABET — THE ABCs OF PREHISTORIC BEASTS
BY MICHELLE HASSELIUS ILLUSTRATED BY CLAIR ROSSITER

A PIRATE ALPHABET — THE ABCs OF PIRACY!
BY ANNA BUTZER ILLUSTRATED BY CHRIS JEVONS

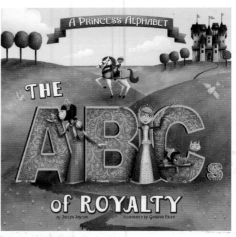

A PRINCESS ALPHABET — THE ABCs of ROYALTY
BY JACLYN JAYCOX ILLUSTRATED BY GUSTAVO ERIZA